The Cats of

Laughing Thunder

Guide For Kids Starting A Business

S. S. Curtis

For Dave and Shiloh

Contents

Chapter 1

Introduction

"If you can dream it, you can do it."

– Walt Disney, co-founder of Disney

Did you know that there are kid **entrepreneurs**? An entrepreneur is someone who creates a business and operates it.

Maybe you've heard of Robert Nay.

No?

Well, in 2010, at 14 years old, Robert created *"Bubble Ball."* This is a mobile game that ended up surpassing *"Angry Birds"* for the most downloaded free game on Apple.

Robert didn't know anything about business or coding, but he knew he wanted to learn, so he did. He learned what he needed at the library and built *"Bubble Ball."* And, he did all this in about a month.

This is just one example of how kids all over the world become entrepreneurs.

Think of a lemonade stand in the summer or maybe your neighbors hire you to shovel snow for them in the winter. Believe it or not, these can be actual businesses.

Do you have an idea for a business? If you do, that's great! Congratulations!

But, while having an idea is amazing, what comes next? How do you take your idea and make it fly? How do you make it a real business?

Well, the first step is to answer the big five questions of what, who, when, where, and how.

Once you have the answers to these questions, you will be able to form a business plan.

This book will help you answer those questions and create a business plan.

For those of you who want to start a business, but don't know what type of business you want to operate, check out Chapters 2 and 17 of this book for some ideas.

(Fritz, Pumpkin, Sven, and Yolanda:
Welcome to Laughing Thunder!)

Chapter 2

What

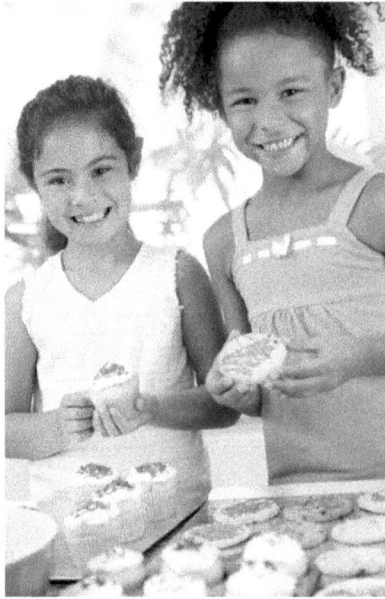

"Build something you're passionate about. As an entrepreneur, you have to have the passion and drive to stay the course."

– Alexandra Chong, founder of *Lulu*

You have a stupendous idea for a business. This idea should include the WHAT.

But, if your dream to start a business doesn't include the WHAT yet, it's time to make your first decision.

What product or service will your business offer?

Below is a list of some *things* you can turn into a business:

Talents

Do you have any talents?

Perhaps you're good at programming and want to write code as your business.

Maybe you play a mean guitar and want to teach neighborhood children as your business.

Get the idea? If you're good at something, you can turn it into a business.

Interests

Another area to think about is what you like. What do you find interesting?

Do you enjoy decorating cakes? Even if you don't have master level skills, you might be able to do simple cake decorating jobs as your business.

As you get more experience, you will be able to perform more advanced cake decorating jobs.

Do you enjoy growing plants and vegetables in your yard? You might be able to do gardening for your neighbors.

Ideas

A few examples of businesses that kids have started are: child care, recycling, bike repair, computer installation, dog walking, crafting, plant sitting, web design, cleaning, energy audits, car washing, word processing, yard work, party planner, and music teacher.

Please look at Chapter 17 for more ideas.

Problem You Are Solving

Once you have chosen a product or service, identify the problem that your product or service solves.

For example, perhaps your music lessons solve the problem of parents having to drive their children to lessons. You go to the home of the music student to give the lesson.

Safety

Whatever product or service you decide to offer, always practice safety. Keep your parents informed of all of your activities and follow their directions.

(Hi, it's Yolanda: I haven't given up on my robot business yet. I just have to solve the bug that causes my robot to keep saying succotash.)

Chapter 3

Who

"I grew up in a small town in Wisconsin. I never thought I'd be where I am."

– Carol Bartz, founder of *Autodesk*

Okay, you've decided on your product or service. Now, it's on to the WHO phase.

WHO will be a part of that business.

Will you be the only one in your business?

Or, will you have other people involved as either partners or employees?

How your business will be structured is an important decision to make.

Sometimes it's nice to have a back-up person so that if one person is sick or busy, there's someone else who can do the work.

When deciding on the WHO of your business, don't expect your parents to do the work for you!

(Fritz, Pumpkin, Sven, and Yolanda: Each of us received business help from our friends. For example, Pumpkin did the videos for Sven's cooking shows!)

Chapter 4

Where

"What do you need to start a business? Three simple things: know your product better than anyone. Know your customer, and have a burning desire to succeed."

- Dave Thomas, founder of *Wendy's*

Things are coming into place. You have the idea and you know who will be involved.

The next step is to decide if you will do the work at your home or at the homes of other people.

Away From Home

If you will work outside of your home, how will you get to the work location? For example, will you walk or ride a bike?

At Home

If you will work at home, will you work in your bedroom, the kitchen, or another room?

Safety

For all work locations, please keep your parents informed of what you're doing, and always be sure to practice safety.

(This is Sven: Of course, my cooking show was produced in my kitchen, one of my favorite places. Yum!)

Chapter 5

When

"Anything you can imagine probably is doable, you just have to imagine it and work on it."

– Larry Page, co-founder of *Google*

You have the WHAT, WHO, and WHERE, now it's on to the WHEN.

Will your business be seasonal? Will it be offered every week? How much time will you be able to spend on your business?

Let's look at some of these considerations.

<u>Season</u>

Is this a business that you will only do at certain times of the year? This is called a seasonal business.

For example, you may have a snow-shoveling business. This is something that only be done during the winter.

Or, maybe you will do gardening. If you live in an area that has four seasons, you will work during the spring and summer.

Another example might be a holiday business – maybe you will sew Halloween costumes.

You might also decide that you only want to operate your business in the summer while you're on vacation from school.

Year Round

If your business can be done in any season, you will have a year-round business.

Examples of some year-round businesses are babysitting, programming, photography, and videography.

Days and Time of Day

Will you work on your business only on the weekend? Or will you work on your business during the school week?

Will you work on your business in the morning, afternoon, or evening?

Hours

You have many responsibilities with school, family, and activities. How many hours can you spend on your business?

Will you need to make changes to make time for your business?

For example, maybe you can spend less time watching television, playing video games, or being on social media.

(Note from Pumpkin: I worked on my "How to be Unmannerly" site before and after school.)

Chapter 6

How

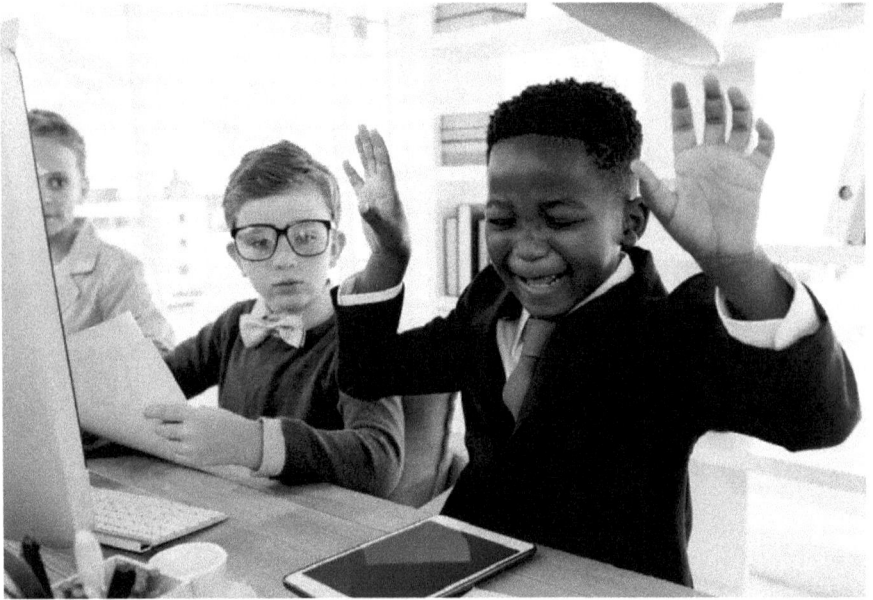

"Whether you think you can or whether you think you can't, you're right!"

– Henry Ford, founder of *Ford Motor Company*

The HOW is the last step in getting started.

How do you plan to provide your product or service?

Here are some things to think about:

<u>Online or In Person</u>

You might decide to make candles, jewelry, or another product and sell it on Etsy.

Or, you might decide to tutor students in person or give music lessons in person.

<u>One Time or Subscription</u>

Other things to think about include the way you plan to offer your product or service.

You might decide to sell one product at a time – for example, one bouquet of balloons for a one-time price.

Or you might decide to provide your service on a subscription basis – for example, you agree to maintain a real estate company's computer system for a fee each month.

(Note from Pumpkin: "Just get on with doing your business! I knew my "How to be Unmannerly" website would be a hit, and I didn't let anyone discourage me.)

Chapter 7

Business Plan – Market Research

"I feel that luck is preparation meeting opportunity."

– Oprah Winfrey, founder of *Harpo Productions*

Now that you have the basic information about your business in place, it's time to think about a plan for your business.

To begin your business plan, you should research the market for your business.

The **market** is a term for the people who will be interested in your business – the people who can benefit from your business. These are the people who will possibly pay you for your service or product.

Research can be done online or in person. (Whenever you are online, please practice safety. You should be supervised by an adult, you should stay out of chat rooms, and you should use filtering software to block unsuitable content.)

You will want to learn about your potential customers and identify your competitors (other dog walking businesses in your community).

For example, you've taken dog obedience training classes and have a lot of experience with dog behavior, so you're interested in a dog walking business. Any potential customer for your business will need to own a dog. Your county might require dogs to be licensed. If so, then you could research your market by going to the county courthouse to get a list of dog license holders in your community.

(Hi, it's Yolanda: Don't be afraid to serve new markets – that's what I did with my Tuxedo Cat Society business. Nobody had paid proper attention to tuxedo cats before. There are a lot of us!)

Chapter 8

Business Plan – Features of Product or Service

"Quality is more important than quantity. One home run is much better than two doubles."

– Steve Jobs, founder of Apple

The next element of your business plan focuses on the features and benefits of your product or service from a customer's point of view.

What's special about your product or service?

What does your product or service do for the customer?

Let's continue with the dog walking example. Your business might be special because you will walk each dog individually in the dog's usual neighborhood park. These facts about your business may be important to many dog owners.

(Fritz's comment: My cloud seeding adventure resulted in some great footage for my weather blog. Viewers loved it!)

Chapter 9

Business Plan – Competitors

"If you think you're too small to have an impact, try going to bed with a mosquito."

– Anita Roddick, founder of *The Body Shop*

Another element of your business plan is to consider other businesses that do what you do – your business **competitors**.

You've determined who they are in your research. But, now you need to determine how you're different from them.

In the dog walking example from the previous chapter, there might be another dog walker (Competitor B) operating in your community.

Maybe Competitor B walks more than one dog at one time. Also, Competitor B doesn't walk any of the dogs at their own neighborhood park.

Your business is different from Competitor B in two important ways: 1) by the number of dogs you walk at one time, and 2) by the park in which you walk the dogs.

(Side note from Pumpkin: Enough of all this dog talk! Cats rule, dogs drool. End of story.)

Chapter 10

Business Plan – Marketing

"Without promotion, something terrible happens – nothing!"

– P.T. Barnum, founder of
Barnum & Bailey's Circus

Marketing is an important element of your business. It's how you let the world know about your business and there are many ways to do this.

Name

Marketing starts with the name. What will be the name of your business? Is the name unique? Is the name easy to remember? Is the name easy to pronounce?

Another thing to consider when deciding on a business name is to have a ***keyword*** in it.

A keyword is a word or phrase that people use to search online for something they want or need.

Going back to the dog walking business, you would want "dog walking" or "dog walker" in the name of your business. The reason for this is so when a dog owner in your community searches online for dog walker, they may come upon your website.

Advertising

You may want to advertise your business online or in a newspaper.

Social Media

You may also want to have your own business website and feature your business in social media (Twitter, Instagram, etc.).

Email

You may also want to send out emails to market your business. If you have a lawn care business, then you might want to email your neighbors to tell them what your business can do for them.

Just be careful with email marketing, as there are new regulations in place to make sure the people you email agree to having you email them. Nobody likes spam.

In Person

Another option is to tell potential customers in person about your business.

You might use your computer to create a **flyer** – a piece of paper with information about your business that you will hand out. Some store owners may allow you to place your flyers in their stores. It can't hurt to ask.

It would also be a good idea to have **business cards.** These cards should have your name and the name of your business along with what you do and how customers can contact you. Hand them out where ever and whenever you can. In fact, you should always have business cards with you so that you are ready to **network** with people you meet.

<u>Sampling</u>

Or, you might decide to offer a small free **sample** of your product or service to encourage customers to buy.

An example of this for a dog walking business might be to offer one free 'mini dog walk' to a potential customer. For this offer, you might walk the dog around the block.

<u>Happy Customers</u>

Hopefully, once you start providing a product or service to your customers, your customers will be pleased. Happy customers will give you

favorable reviews online or by word-of-mouth. They may even refer other customers to you!

Happy customers are the most precious assets of any business.

<u>Expenses</u>

All of this marketing may cost some money. You will need to decide what your budget for marketing will be. You will also need to keep track of all of your marketing expenses.

(Note from Pumpkin: Your business should definitely have a website – that's the secret of my success. That, and excellent sound effects.)

Chapter 11

Business Plan - Pricing

"Any business plan won't survive its first encounter with reality. The reality will always be different. It will never be the plan."

– Jeff Bezos, founder of *Amazon*

If you're going to sell a product or a service, you need know what you're going to charge the customer.

There are lots of different pricing strategies you can follow. Below are a few.

Premium or Value

One of the first things to consider is that your pricing should reflect your product.

For example, if you go into the business of producing organic cat food, you should charge a higher price (called a **premium pricing strategy**) than you would for non-organic cat food.

On the flip side, if you decide to produce non-organic cat food, you would charge a lower price (called a **value pricing strategy**).

Competitors

Next, you should compare your prices with your competitors.

Suppose you're going to wash cars for your neighbors at your house. Your competitor might be a commercial car wash five miles away that charges $10 per car wash. Your neighbors might be willing to pay more since your business is located much closer to them – so you decide to charge $12.50 for a car wash.

Other Things to Consider

Another important element of setting your prices is to consider your costs (expenses) for operating your business. You want your business to be a money-maker, not a money-loser!

(Hi, Yolanda again: Membership fees and event tickets were the keys to my money-making Tuxedo Cat Society business.)

Chapter 12

Business Plan – Production

"It's the building of things that makes you happy."

– Caterina Fake, co- founder of *Flickr and Hunch*

Along with the other elements in your business plan, you will need to decide how you will make or produce your product? If your business involves a service, how do you plan to perform or deliver your service?

Product

Let's define a **product** before we get into this. A product is a tangible (physical) item that you sell.

Okay, so let's say that your business involves selling plush stuffed marine animal toys. Will you sew the toys yourself? Or, will you buy the toys from someone else, decorate them yourself, and then sell them?

If you buy the toys from someone else, you will need to find that person or business (called your **supplier**). You will also need to find out the supplier's pricing and payment terms. The difference between the price that the supplier charges you and the price that you will charge your customers is called your **margin**.

You will need to subtract all of your expenses and costs from your margin to get your **profit**.

Also, how many toys will you have on hand to sell? The number of toys is called your *inventory*.

Service

A **service** on the other hand is something you do for someone else that you get paid for.

Suppose your business is mowing lawns. You will need to have a lawn mower to move to the yard you will be mowing.

If you will be mowing lawns in your neighborhood, then moving between yards will be easy.

If you will be mowing lawns all over your community, then you will have to consider how to move the lawn mower to each job.

(This is Sven: Yes, this cat food example is a good business possibility. I may have to consider that myself. I imagine a tasty, premium cat food – none of this low-rent junk.)

Chapter 13

Business Plan – Start-Up Expenses

"If you would like to know the value of money, try to borrow some."

– Benjamin Franklin; businessman, inventor, writer, diplomat

You've done all the planning – congratulations! Now you're ready to start your business.

<u>Start-Up Expenses</u>

There is an old saying that "it takes money to make money."

Before you receive any money from your customers, you will usually have some **start-up expenses**.

Let's use a simple lemonade stand as an example.

You've got to have lemons and sugar to make the lemonade, right? That's an expense.

You will also need cups for your customers to drink the lemonade. They can be paper cups or cups from your home that you will then have to wash (oh-oh, you will need some soap for washing those cups as well). Another expense.

Then there's paper and markers to make a sign to advertise your lemonade stand. Cha-ching.

Hopefully, your family will allow you to use a pitcher, a spoon, and a table from your home.

Before you're able to make a penny from selling your lemonade, you will have had to spend some money in start-up expenses.

Source of Funding

So, now you know you will most likely need some money to start your business, but where will you get the money? What will be the source of money for your start-up expenses?

Do you have savings that you will use?

Or, will you get a loan from someone?

Most lenders will not give you a loan without requiring you to pay back more than the amount of the loan. This extra amount is called **interest**. If you borrow $10, then you may be required to pay back $10.60 – the original $10 amount of the loan plus the interest of $.60.

Or, will you get an investment from someone?

Most investors will not make an investment without requiring something in return. For example, investors may require that they own some part of your business in return for investing in it.

(Fritz's comment: I used money I received for my birthday as well as my allowance.)

Chapter 14

Business Plan – Profit

"What I wanted was to be allowed to do the thing in the world that I did best – which I believe then and believe now is the greatest privilege there is. When I did that, success found me."

– Debbie Fields, founder of *Mrs. Fields Cookies*

You've got all your business ducks in a row.

You've figured out your expenses and have the money you need to get started.

Next up is actually starting your business and making money (a **profit**).

So, what exactly is a profit?

Let's go over a couple of business terms before we get to that question:

Revenue is the income (money) made by your business from selling goods or services.

Expenses are the dollars you spend to run the business. Examples of expenses are the costs of materials (might be the stuffing for your stuffed animals), supplies (might be notepads), equipment (might be the sewing machine needed to sew the stuffed animals), etc.

A **profit** is when the revenue is greater than all the expenses.

If the expenses are greater than the revenue, then you have a **loss**. This means you are losing money.

To figure out if you're making a profit, add up all your revenue then subtract all your expenses. The difference is your profit or loss.

Keep good records of all of your revenue and expenses so it will be easy for you to know if your business is making a profit.

If you're not making a profit, go over your business plan again. Try to figure out what the problem is.

Let's go back to the stuffed animal business as an example.

Suppose the cost of making one stuffed animal is $4.25.

You're charging the customer $3.99 for that stuffed animal.

Do you see the problem? Your cost is more than your revenue.

You need to increase the price of your product to more than it costs you to make. You might charge the customer $4.50 per stuffed animal.

(Hi, it's Yolanda: I kept close track of my revenue and expenses so that I know I made a good profit from the Tuxedo Cat Society membership fees and event tickets.)

Chapter 15

Business Plan
– Government

"You only have to do a very few things right in your life so long as you don't do too many things wrong."

– Warren Buffet, investor

Yep, when it comes to a business, kids have to follow the same rules as adults.

To make sure you are doing everything right, you will need to check with your city or county to see if your business requires a local *license*.

Also, as of the printing of this book, if you earn more than $400 from your business in one year, you will need to file your own *income tax* return. The amount of income tax you will owe will depend on how much you earn, as well as any other income you might have such as interest on a savings account.

In addition to income tax, you will need to pay *self-employment tax*. You should put aside about 15% of the total amount you earn from your business before expenses to cover self-employment tax.

Be sure to talk to your family for help with these important matters.

(This is Sven: Taxes are a major annoyance. Thank goodness my mother is an expert on taxes and can help me.)

Chapter 16

Tips

"It was a risk . . . But I don't look at risk the way other people do. When you're an entrepreneur, you have to go in feeling like you're going to be successful."

– Lillian Vernon, founder of
Lillian Vernon Corporation

The Cats of Laughing Thunder want to help you with your business. They don't want you to have some of the problems they did! Check out their book *The Cats of Laughing Thunder in The New Businesses Adventure* for more details.

Let's look at a couple of their mistakes.

<u>Not Enough Monitoring</u>

In Chapter 12 of *The New Businesses Adventure*, Sven admits he doesn't know how many viewers his cooking show has on YouTube. This is important information. His lame excuse is that he's been too busy inventing new dishes.

Sven should know that each viewer is a potential customer. On the flip side, if no one is watching his videos, then he might consider stopping the videos and spending time on another marketing idea.

<u>Not Enough Planning</u>

Yolanda has a different problem in Chapters 10 and 11 of *The New Businesses Adventure*. She hasn't prepared well enough for the first meeting of the Tuxedo Cat Society, so there are not enough activities for all of the cats.

Word of mouth is a BIG marketing strategy. You want your customers to be happy with your services so they will tell their friends and others. This will help your business grow.

Not Enough Focus on Profit

Profit is key for any business, but Fritz neglects this fact in Chapter 9 of *The New Businesses Adventure*. He needs advertisers for his weather blog in order to make a profit. His problem is that he didn't think through how to get those advertisers.

Not Enough Family Support

Pumpkin has a *"How to be Unmannerly"* website in Chapter 6 of *The New Businesses Adventure*. However, his grandmother has her own manners business, and she is not happy with Pumpkin's website.

Tips - Do This

Act Like a Professional

With his cooking show, Sven did a professional job of being a chef. Each dish featured was planned carefully (even if some of the dishes might not appeal to humans).

Because he was prepared, he got rave reviews. This is good for business.

Be Serious About Your Business

Cats with tuxedo markings on their fur were neglected in Yolanda's view. So she set up a business to serve those cats, the Tuxedo Cat Society. She charged for membership and activities. She focused on keeping expenses low.

Because she was serious about her business revenue and expenses, she was able to earn a profit.

Have Knowledge About Your Business

Fritz had both interest in and knowledge of meteorology. So, he had a good background for his weather blog business. This helped his business succeed.

Save Most of Your Profits

Pumpkin's *"How to be Unmannerly"* website generated a lot of advertising money. Pumpkin wisely put most of his profits in his college savings account.

(Fritz, Pumpkin, Sven, and Yolanda:
Good luck with your business!)

Chapter 17

Business Ideas

"You have brains in your head. You have feet in your shoes. You can steer yourself, any direction you choose."

– Dr. Seuss

If you don't have your own ideas for a business, below are a few business ideas to get you thinking. But, don't feel these are the only things you can do. Your imagination is limitless!

Administrative (file, letters, post office, etc.)

Art (paint, draw, sculpt, etc.)

Babysitting (mother's helper, babysitter, etc.)

Beauty (cut hair, perm hair, color hair, manicure nails, etc.)

Crafts (jewelry, accessories, home décor, etc.)

Computers (install, update, web service consulting, program, etc.)

Delivery (walk, bike, skateboard, etc.)

Design (any thing)

Electronics (install, repair, assemble, advise, etc.)

Farming (plants, animals)

Fashion (alter, repair, sew, etc.)

Foreign Languages (teach, translate, etc.)

Gardening (includes lawn mowing, weeding, planting, etc.)

Holidays (buy gifts, wrap gifts, decorate, etc.)

House Cleaning (general maid service, specific cleaning tasks, etc.)

Lemonade Stand

Music (teach, perform, compose, etc.)

Organizing (closets, attics, basements, garages, garage sales, etc.)

Pets (walking, sitting, training, etc.)

Photo/Video (events, pets, kids, etc.)

Sports (teach, coach, referee, etc.)

Teaching (any subject, homework help, tutoring, etc.)

Writing (help manual, advertising, blog, etc.)

(Fritz, Pumpkin, Sven, and Yolanda:
Stay safe out there!)

Also by S. S. Curtis:

The Cats of Laughing Thunder in
The New Businesses Adventure

The Cats of Laughing Thunder in
The Nasty Gray Adventure

Coming soon:

Fritz's Book of Weather Favorites

The Cats of Laughing Thunder in
The Moaning House Adventure

Excerpt from The Cats of Laughing Thunder in The New Businesses Adventure – Chapter 5

Fritz's Weather Blog

Wednesday, March 15:

Weather Forecast for Josheka Farm, Laughing Thunder County, Minnesota - Mostly clear but cooler with a high of 32 degrees Fahrenheit

Fritz, Pumpkin, Sven, and Yolanda met the following morning.

"Thank the Great Cat it's teacher-in-service day, so we don't have Cat School," said Fritz. "My blimp's arrived and I need your help."

"What are we going to do?" asked Pumpkin.

"There's an ice jam on the Upper Lower

River," said Fritz. "I need to make a video of it for my website."

The cats climbed aboard the blimp.

"Ready for takeoff!" said Fritz.

Up the blimp went.

"Yolanda, help me with the weather instruments. Sven, steer the blimp. Pumpkin, shoot video," said Fritz.

Soon they were over the Upper Lower River.

"Wow, look at the flooding upstream!" said Fritz. "Look at the huge chunks of ice on the river banks!"

The cats gazed out the windows at the sight. The ice chunks were at least eight feet tall.

"It's the Ice Age again!" said Pumpkin.

Sven was so busy looking at the ice that he forgot to steer.

Crunch! Crash! Scrape!

The cats were thrown out of their seats, but Pumpkin managed to keep his camera recording. Fritz pushed himself off the floor. He had a barometer hanging around one ear.

"By the Great Cat, what happened?" asked Fritz.

The cats peered out the windows.

"We appear to be stuck in a giant oak tree," said Yolanda.

Fritz grabbed the controls. He pushed the control stick forward. He pushed the control stick backward. He did this three times.

Finally, the blimp pulled free from the tree.

"Sven, your time as pilot is over. I'll fly us home," Fritz said.

About the Author

S. S. Curtis's father started her in business when she was five years old by giving her a beef calf to raise. Her next business venture was raising baby pigs with her brother. On the side, she did a little babysitting. After earning B.A., M.B.A., and J.D. degrees, she worked in different roles in the fields of technology, law, and consumer goods. She is a co-founder of ThinkerBlox, LLC. Her child also started a business at the age of five (making and selling Christmas ornaments), and is now pursuing business adventures in robotics.

S. S. Curtis is the author of the Cats of Laughing Thunder series of fiction and non-fiction books for children. You can explore the world of Laughing Thunder at

http://www.laughingthunder.com.

www.ingramcontent.com/pod-product-compliance
Lightning Source LLC
Chambersburg PA
CBHW060641210326
41520CB00010B/1689